THE GIRL WHO
TESTED THE WATERS

ELLEN SWALLOW, ENVIRONMENTAL SCIENTIST

*To James and Luke,
and to all the "earnest seekers"
of the past, present, and future*

PD

THE GIRL WHO TESTED THE WATERS

ELLEN SWALLOW, ENVIRONMENTAL SCIENTIST

Patricia Daniele

illustrated by Junyi Wu

mit Kids Press

ELLEN HENRIETTA SWALLOW arrived in the world in 1842, tiny as a bird, with lungs that could hardly pump air. "Fresh air and exercise," her doctor declared. "That's what Ellen needs to grow strong!"

Following the doctor's orders, her mother took her outside, though she hovered like a hen protecting her chick. Year by year, tiny Ellen, nourished by nature's remedies of fresh air, fresh food, and clean sparkling water on the family farm in northern Massachusetts, grew stronger both in body and in mind.

She loved being outside, even when winter winds whipped at her nose or summer sun scorched her bonnet.

An only child, she was expected to help with the farm chores. Each morning, with skirt swishing, Ellen hopped into the driver's seat of their farm wagon. With a *click* and a *tsk*, she drove the horses to the hayfield. *Swish . . . thunk . . . swish*. She hoisted bales into the wagon. *Thunk . . . scoop . . . thunk . . . scrape*. She shoveled out stalls. She fed and cleaned and helped birth animals.

Chores done, Ellen found a friend in nature and discovered a lifelong love of science in the world outside. She delighted in cultivating her little garden and in collecting, counting, and categorizing every animal, plant, mineral, or fossil she found in the fields. She tramped through the piney woods and splashed in the sparkling brook that ran past the farmhouse.

When it came time to
enroll in school, Mother said
no. She feared Ellen might catch
an illness from the other children.
Instead, the kitchen table became
Ellen's classroom. Her parents, both
teachers, took turns instructing her.

Ellen learned numbers counting apple slices and measuring flour for the pies she helped Mother bake.

Father taught history and logic. Ellen mastered literature by reading with her family by the light of a crackling fire every night.

By the time Ellen was sixteen, her parents had taught her all they knew. But the more Ellen learned, the more she hungered to learn. How would the meager income from the Swallow farm ever be enough to pay for more education for Ellen?

Her parents sold the homestead to Mr. Swallow's brother and piled up their wagon with all they could carry. Ellen said goodbye to the farmhouse and the animals she loved.

The Swallows bought a general store ten miles away and enrolled Ellen in Westford Academy, which sat across the village green from their store.

Every morning, Ellen helped her mother tidy up the house, helped her father open up the store, and sped across the village green to school. Before long, she had taken every subject the school offered and was tutoring fellow students and assisting the teachers in their classes.

But what was next? Most women, in those days, did not go to college, let alone study science and math. But that's what Ellen wanted to do.

One day, while helping her father in the store, she spied a notice in a magazine that made her imagination take flight. It was for a new school for women in upstate New York: Vassar College. But the tuition was three hundred dollars. That amount would buy over three thousand pounds of sugar! Where would a poor girl get so much money?

For the next two years, when her tasks in the store were finished, she scrubbed and dusted houses. She cared for the sick. She did anything to earn tuition. "Tired . . . So tired . . . Busy . . . Tired," she wrote in her diary.

Slowly, the dollars trickled in—enough for one year's tuition.

At twenty-six, she wrote:

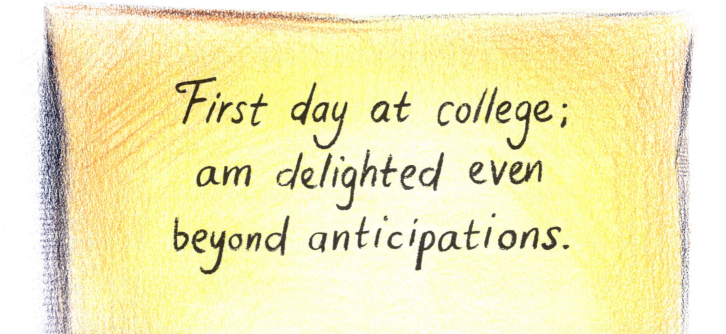

First day at college; am delighted even beyond anticipations.

Ellen never wasted a minute at Vassar. She read while walking to class. She developed her own shorthand to take notes faster. She earned a scholarship and she tutored other students, earning an average of a whopping $1.50 a day—as much as a woman working in a factory made in a week—to pay the next year's expenses and tuition.

At first, Ellen wanted to study astronomy—the galaxies, stars, and planets. But a class in applied chemistry changed her life. It was more down to earth. It used science to solve the problems of everyday life—contaminated food and polluted water and air. She jumped at the chance to be outdoors again, collecting, counting, categorizing, and measuring.

Ellen analyzed anything she could get her hands on—from soil and water to baking powder and boot blacking. She measured, weighed, and examined her samples under microscopes to see what they were composed of. Ellen would measure the contents of a dustpan, one classmate said.

Upon completing college, she made up her mind to be a chemist and boldly applied to all the big chemical companies. None had ever hired a woman. "I have tried several doors . . . and they won't open," she wrote to a friend. A chemist from one company suggested she apply to the new Massachusetts Institute of Technology for further studies.

Every student at MIT was male. Ellen didn't care. She applied anyway and got in—with a full scholarship! The year was 1871. At twenty-eight years old, Ellen Henrietta Swallow was about to become the first female student to step through the doors of MIT.

But not everybody liked change.

MIT students and professors complained and grumbled and grumbled and complained: Why "should a female take up scientific studies reserved for men? Woman's place is in the home . . . and if one woman is admitted, others will follow."

When she arrived, she was directed to go down, down, down to the basement lab and her "special" desk. There was not another chair or student in sight, nor were there any professors.

Ellen stared at the empty room. She didn't know her free tuition had come at a price. The school called her admission "the Swallow Experiment." She wasn't allowed in class with the men, so if she failed, they could claim she was never admitted as a student.

Ellen dared not fail.

The professors slid Ellen's lessons under the door of her basement lab and picked them up the next day when she'd completed them. For over a year, Ellen studied chemistry this way, but in time, she impressed her professors and classmates and was allowed to take classes with them.

One day, she was bent over a microscope when a professor
summoned her to his office. But Ellen hadn't done anything wrong.

Her professor, despite his misgivings about a woman student, had
seen Ellen excel in his classes, and he needed the best student to work on
a water survey for the city of Boston.

The flow of water through the city could not keep pace with the flow of arriving immigrants. What little water ran through the city became clogged with garbage and ripe with the smell of sewage. Textile mills, breweries, and factories dumped dyes, heavy metals, poison, and disease-causing bacteria into the city's lakes, rivers, and ponds. Epidemics of cholera, typhoid, and diarrheal diseases were spreading through the water supply. Polluted drinking water was making many people sick.

People were dying.

Toxic waters needed to be identified.

Safe, clean sources of water had to be found.

Ellen seized the opportunity to put her education to use. Her task was to collect water samples from all over the Boston area and analyze them quickly.

People stared as Ellen, in all kinds of weather, scrambled over slippery rocks, bent over muddy rivers and streams, and collected thousands of samples throughout the city and surrounding neighborhoods. With her bags full of small bottles, Ellen hurried back to the lab. The water had to be analyzed within a few hours of being collected or it was useless.

Hour after hour, Ellen analyzed the water one bottle at a time, first shaking it, removing the stopper, then sniffing it. The odor of ammonia was a clue it contained sewage material.

Next, she poured, measured, filtered, heated, weighed, and mixed, testing the water sample for ammonia and nitrates, more hints the water contained refuse. Then she analyzed the water for minerals and organic matter, a sure sign sewage had been dumped in the rivers and streams. She carefully recorded her observations in her notebooks.

For two years, she worked seven days a week, often late into the night until her eyes blurred and her body ached for rest. Sometimes she got only four hours of sleep a night. After one late-night session, she looked at all the bottles of water that still needed examining. Her shoulders slumped. She wished she were triplets.

After testing twenty thousand samples, Ellen had done it! With unwavering persistence, she proved which rivers and streams contained pollution and which ones were clean. Her professor delivered her detailed findings to the Massachusetts Board of Health.

Even before she graduated from MIT, Ellen became one of
the world's renowned water analysts. After she completed a
second groundbreaking study, Massachusetts built the
first water treatment plant, and the number of deaths of
children and their family members went down.

Her work led Massachusetts to establish the first
water quality standards in the country. Other
states and countries followed its example.

Ellen didn't stop at water.

With no laws controlling it, unsanitary food was making its way to the dinner table.

Ellen traveled all over the state buying sacks of groceries to test. She found spoiled meat, salt added to flour, sawdust in cinnamon, and hundreds of other mislabeled groceries. Ellen pressed for change, and Massachusetts eventually passed the first pure food laws in the country.

Ellen came to think of her approach to improving living conditions as a new kind of science and borrowed a German term to describe it: *ecology*. She saw it as the study of how people and organisms relate to one another and the environment. She believed it was essential for all branches of science to work together to find solutions for environmental problems—for the sake of people now and for future generations.

At the time, many scientists rejected her ideas, but that didn't stop her. She took a different approach and brought environmental science to homes and schools through the American Home Economics Association. She served as the organization's first president and taught the public, both adults and children, how to lead healthier lives by caring for their homes and environment.

Ellen remembered how as a child, fresh air, clean water, and healthful food had made her strong, and she worked tirelessly for the rest of her life applying "the facts . . . of science" to the problems of everyday life to create a safer environment for others.

After Ellen died, her biographer wrote, "Her life goes on in a thousand forms and in a thousand places." Ellen's work spread like ripples in a pond, inspiring future generations to follow her lead and continue the fight for clean water and a healthy environment.

"*The quality of life depends on the ability of society to teach its members how to live in harmony with their environment—defined first as the family, then with the community, then with the world and its resources.*"

—Ellen Swallow

"*She was among the first to realize the necessity for technology to counteract its own effects.*"

—Jerome B. Wiesner, president of MIT, 1971–1980

TIME LINE

———

1842   Ellen Swallow is born on December 3 in Dunstable, Massachusetts.

1859   Her father sells the family's farm to a brother and buys a general store to earn more for Ellen's education at Westford Academy.

1868   Begins attending Vassar College, in upstate New York.

1870   Graduates from Vassar.

1871   Becomes the first woman student at the Massachusetts Institute of Technology.

1872   Begins testing water samples in the Boston area.

1873   Graduates from MIT.

1875   Marries Professor Robert Richards.

1876   Opens the Women's Laboratory at MIT, where she begins teaching women students, who are classified as "special students."

1878　Works with her students to begin a comprehensive analysis of contaminated foods, which will prompt Massachusetts and Connecticut to pass pure food and drug laws.

1884　Is appointed an instructor at MIT.

1887　Conducts a second water study in the Boston area and maps out sources of polluted water and clean water, leading to the nation's first water quality standards.

1892　Introduces a new field of environmental science, oekology (ecology), a term coined by Ernst Haeckel, at the Vendome Hotel in Boston.

1908　Becomes the first president of the American Home Economics Association and founds the *Journal of Home Economics*.

1910　Is granted an honorary doctor of science degree from Smith College, having been denied one from MIT.

1911　Dies of heart failure on March 30 at age sixty-eight.

1911　The Ellen Richards Research Prize, the first science prize awarded to women, is created after her death.

1915　The Ecological Society of America is formed.

AUTHOR'S NOTE

My admiration for Ellen Swallow began many years ago when my husband, Joe, was a student at MIT. I never realized then that I would write a book about this remarkable woman who was decades ahead of her time. Over the years, and as I dug into her life in the archives at MIT, in Dunstable (her birthplace), and in the books I read about her, I was excited to discover that she had accomplished much more than just being the first woman accepted at MIT.

In addition to her tireless work as a water analyst, she was an advocate for women's education. Before she became an instructor at MIT, she set up the Women's Laboratory in a run-down garage called "the dump." It was the first lab of its kind in the world. With the approval of the governing board of MIT, she taught classes there for no pay and raised money for supplies and equipment. Seven years and five hundred students later, the lab closed when MIT became officially coed. Since that time, thousands of female graduates and faculty members have followed in Ellen's footsteps.

Ellen's legacy has lived on since then, sometimes in surprising ways. In 1951, DC Comics featured her in the series Wonder Women of History, which celebrated women who succeeded through hard work rather than

superpowers. In 2009, President Barack Obama honored her as one of five "Women Taking the Lead to Save Our Planet."

One of Ellen's biggest fans was Robert Hallowell Richards, a professor at MIT. They were extreme opposites. Ellen was small, dark-haired, and quick in mind and body. Robert was tall, light-haired, athletic, and easy-going. Their love of science and of each other made them a perfect pair. They married in 1875 and moved into their home at 32 Eliot Street (now a National Historic Landmark) in the Boston neighborhood of Jamaica Plain. Over the years, the house became a laboratory for teaching and using their scientific knowledge. They enjoyed making it a model for their concept of "right living." It was filled with books, sunlight, and fresh air and supplied with clean, fresh well water. Dusty, heavy draperies and rugs were replaced with plant-filled windows, polished hardwood floors, and skylights.

Ellen earned a considerable amount of money from teaching, patents, writing, consulting, and lecturing, but it was discovered after her death that she had given it all away to help the causes and programs she supported.

Her husband, Robert, had these fitting words inscribed on her gravestone:

Pioneer: Educator, Scientist.
An earnest seeker, a tireless worker.
A faithful friend and helper of mankind.

SOURCE NOTES

p. 13: "Tired . . . So tired . . . Busy . . . Tired": quoted in Hunt, 34.

p. 13: "First day . . . anticipations": ibid., 35.

p. 15: Ellen would measure . . . dustpan: Vare, 30.

p. 16: "I have tried . . . won't open": quoted in Hunt, 83.

p. 17: "should a female . . . will follow": quoted in Clarke, 46.

p. 18: "special" desk: quoted in Swallow, 38.

p. 18: "Swallow Experiment": quoted in Clarke, 24.

p. 26: She wished she were triplets: based on Hunt, 323.

p. 30: "the facts . . . of science": quoted in Stern, 121.

p. 31: "Her life goes on . . . places": quoted in Hunt, 328.

p. 32: "The quality of life . . . its resources": quoted in Swallow, 95.

p. 33: "She was among . . . own effects": ibid., 96.

SELECTED BIBLIOGRAPHY

Breton, Mary Joy. *Women Pioneers for the Environment*. Boston: Northeastern University Press, 2000.

Clarke, Robert. *Ellen Swallow: The Woman Who Founded Ecology*. Chicago: Follett, 1973.

Douty, Esther Morris. *America's First Woman Chemist, Ellen Richards*. New York: Julian Messner, 1961.

Hunt, Caroline Louisa. *The Life of Ellen H. Richards*. Boston: Whitcomb & Barrows, 1912.

Massachusetts Institute of Technology Archives, Cambridge, MA. https://archivesspace.mit.edu/.

Musil, Robert K. *Rachel Carson and Her Sisters*. New Brunswick, NJ: Rutgers University Press, 2015.

Nichols, William Ripley. *On the Present Condition of Certain Rivers of Massachusetts, Together with Considerations Touching the Water Supply of Towns*. Boston: Massachusetts Board of Health, 1874.

Stern, Madeleine B. "The First Woman Graduate of MIT: Ellen H. Richards." In *We the Women: Career Firsts of Nineteenth-Century America*. Lincoln, NE: University of Nebraska Press, 1994.

Swallow, Pamela Curtis. *The Remarkable Life and Career of Ellen Swallow Richards*. Hoboken, NJ: Wiley, 2014.

Sweetser, Kate. "Ellen Richards: A Girl Who Loved Science." In *Great American Girls*. New York: Dodd Mead, 1931.

Vare, Ethlie Ann. *Adventurous Spirit: A Story about Ellen Swallow Richards*. Minneapolis: Carolrhoda Books, 1992.

ACKNOWLEDGMENTS

My deepest gratitude to my husband, Joe, and the rest of my family; Anne Bromley, my critique partner; Sarah Stephens, my agent; Kristin Zelazko and Lydia Abel, my editors; and everyone at Candlewick and MIT Kids Press for their encouragement, support, and insights.

PATRICIA DANIELE is an avid reader and likes to dig into and write stories about can-do people who have dared to overcome obstacles, succeeded, and inspired others. Growing up in New England, she spent summers swimming in the cold waves of the Atlantic Ocean. A mother of two grown boys, she now lives with her husband on the West Coast and enjoys swimming in the warmer Pacific Ocean waves near her home.

JUNYI WU is an illustrator from Southern California. Like Ellen Swallow, she loves gardening, exploring the outdoors, and collecting natural finds such as rocks and wildflowers.

Text copyright © 2025 by Patricia Daniele. Illustrations copyright © 2025 by Junyi Wu. All rights reserved. No part of this book may be reproduced, transmitted, or stored in an information retrieval system in any form or by any means, graphic, electronic, or mechanical, including photocopying, taping, and recording, without prior written permission from the publisher. The MIT Press, the ☰mit Kids Press colophon, and MIT Kids Press are trademarks of The MIT Press, a department of the Massachusetts Institute of Technology, and used under license from The MIT Press. The colophon and MIT Kids Press are registered in the US Patent and Trademark Office. First edition 2025. Library of Congress Catalog Card Number pending. ISBN 978-1-5362-3005-5. This book was typeset in Garamond Premier Pro. The illustrations were done in colored pencil. MIT Kids Press, an imprint of Candlewick Press, 99 Dover Street, Somerville, Massachusetts 02144. mitkidspress.com. candlewick.com. Printed in Shenzhen, Guangdong, China. 24 25 26 27 28 29 CCP 10 9 8 7 6 5 4 3 2 1